BRINGING BACK THE

American Alligator

Cynthia O'Brien

CRABTREE
PUBLISHING COMPANY
WWW.CRABTREEBOOKS.COM

CRABTREE
PUBLISHING COMPANY
WWW.CRABTREEBOOKS.COM

Author: Cynthia O'Brien

Series Research and Development: Reagan Miller

Managing Editor: Tim Cooke

Picture Manager: Sophie Mortimer

Design Manager: Keith Davis

Editorial Director: Lindsey Lowe

Children's Publisher: Anne O'Daly

Editor: Janine Deschenes

Proofreader: Lorna Notsch

Cover design: Margaret Amy Salter

**Production coordinator and
Prepress technician:** Margaret Amy Salter

Print coordinator: Katherine Berti

Produced for Crabtree Publishing Company
by Brown Bear Books

Photographs (t=top, b= bottom, l=left, r=right, c=center)

Front Cover: All images from Shutterstock

Interior: Alamy: Aurora Photos, 14-15, Rosa Irene Betancourt, 18, Ian Dagnall, 19b, David Fleetham, 6, David Foster, 11t, Barry Lewis, 12, Science History Images, 5b, US Air Force Photo, 19t, Zuma Press Inc, 15; Dreamstime: John Anderson, 27b, Andylid, 24, Sergey Lavrentev, 26, Donnie Shackleford, 21; Getty Images: John Dreyer, 22, Tyrone Turner/National Geographic, 20; iStock: Betty 4240, 28, Clark42, 29, S Goodwin, 5t, Mark Kostich, 1, NaluPhoto, 7, N Nehring, 8, K Senija, 27t, Durk Talsma 25t; Library of Congress: 9t, 9b, 16; Nature Picture Library: Tom Mangelsen, 10; Reuters: 17b; Shutterstock: Sid Dima, 25b, Kiera Heiko, 17t, Martin Mecnarowski, 13b, Susan Montgomery, 13t, Anthony Ricci, 11b, Rudy Umans, 4; USGS: Phil Wilkinson, 23.

Brown Bear Books has made every attempt to contact the copyright holder. If you have any information please contact licensing@brownbearbooks.co.uk

Library and Archives Canada Cataloguing in Publication

O'Brien, Cynthia (Cynthia J.), author
    Bringing back the American alligator / Cynthia O'Brien.

(Animals back from the brink)
Includes index.
Issued in print and electronic formats.
ISBN 978-0-7787-4901-1 (hardcover).--
ISBN 978-0-7787-4907-3 (softcover).--
ISBN 978-1-4271-2101-1 (HTML)

    1. American alligator--Juvenile literature. 2. American alligator--Conservation--Juvenile literature. 3. Endangered species--Juvenile literature. 4. Wildlife recovery--Juvenile literature. I. Title.

QL666.C925O27 2018   j333.95'798416   C2018-903045-3
                                                    C2018-903046-1

Library of Congress Cataloging-in-Publication Data

Names: O'Brien, Cynthia (Cynthia J.), author.
Title: Bringing back the American alligator / Cynthia O'Brien.
Description: New York, New York : Crabtree Publishing, [2019] |
    Series: Animals back from the brink | Includes index.
Identifiers: LCCN 2018036856 (print) | LCCN 2018037478 (ebook) |
    ISBN 9781427121011 (Electronic) |
    ISBN 9780778749011 (hardcover : alk. paper) |
    ISBN 9780778749073 (paperback : alk. paper)
Subjects: LCSH: American alligator--Southern States--Conservation--
    Juvenile literature.
Classification: LCC QL666.C925 (ebook) |
    LCC QL666.C925 O29 2019 (print) | DDC 597.98/4--dc23
LC record available at https://lccn.loc.gov/2018036856

Crabtree Publishing Company
www.crabtreebooks.com   1-800-387-7650

Printed in the U.S.A./102018/CG20180810

**Published in Canada
Crabtree Publishing**
616 Welland Ave.
St. Catharines, Ontario
L2M 5V6

**Published in the United States
Crabtree Publishing**
PMB 59051
350 Fifth Avenue, 59th Floor
New York, New York 10118

**Published in the United Kingdom
Crabtree Publishing**
Maritime House
Basin Road North, Hove
BN41 1WR

**Published in Australia
Crabtree Publishing**
3 Charles Street
Coburg North
VIC, 3058

Contents

Find videos and extra material online at **crabtreeplus.com** to learn more about the conservation of animals and ecosystems. See page 30 in this book for the access code to this material.

The Disappearing Alligator

American alligators have lived on Earth for more than 150 million years. They are the largest **reptiles** in North America. They are **carnivores** that eat fish, birds, frogs, and small animals such as muskrat. When European **settlers** arrived in the South in the 1500s, there were seven million American alligators. By the mid 1900s, the alligator was **endangered**. The population was just 700,000. The alligators' habitat of freshwater rivers, swamps, marshes, and lakes was being destroyed by people. People also hunted alligators in huge numbers.

Until the 1900s, there were millions of alligators swimming in the southeastern **wetlands**. The adult American alligator is an **apex predator** in its **ecosystem**. The main threat to the alligator is from humans.

SPOT THE DIFFERENCE

The American alligator looks so similar to its endangered relative, the American crocodile, that hunters mix them up. In fact, to stop the accidental hunting of the American crocodile, the U.S. government lists the American alligator as "threatened," too. Alligators look similar to crocodiles, but the alligator's snout (right) is shorter and wider than the crocodile's long snout. When an alligator's mouth is closed, no teeth can be seen. A crocodile's large fourth tooth sticks out, even when its mouth is closed. Alligators and crocodiles also live in different **habitats**. Crocodiles live in salt water, whereas alligators need fresh water to live.

American alligators have been hunted for hundreds of years by the Tumucua (above) and Calusa people in what is now Florida. But they never killed more alligators than what they needed. When European settlers arrived, hunting became a problem. It was one of the main reasons the alligator population declined.

Species at Risk

Created in 1984, the International Union for the **Conservation** of Nature (IUCN) protects wildlife, plants, and **natural resources** around the world. Its members include about 1,400 governments and nongovernmental organizations. The IUCN publishes the Red List of Threatened **Species** each year, which tells people how likely a plant or animal species is to become extinct. It began publishing the list in 1964.

The Pinta Island tortoise lived on only one island off the coast of Ecuador. The Red List classified the tortoise as Extinct (EX) in 2016. The IUCN updates the Red List twice a year to track the changing of species. Each individual species is reevaluated at least every five years.

SCIENTIFIC CRITERIA

The Red List, created by scientists, divides nearly 80,000 species of plants and animals into nine categories. Criteria for each category include the growth and **decline** of the population size of a species. They also include how many individuals within a species can breed, or have babies. In addition, scientists include information about the habitat of the species, such as its size and quality. These criteria allow scientists to figure out the probability of extinction facing the species.

IUCN LEVELS OF THREAT

The Red List uses nine categories to define the threat to a species.

Extinct (EX)	No living individuals survive
Extinct in the Wild (EW)	Species cannot be found in its natural habitat. Exists only in **captivity**, in **cultivation**, or in an area that is not its natural habitat.
Critically Endangered (CR)	At extremely high risk of becoming extinct in the wild
Endangered (EN)	At very high risk of extinction in the wild
Vulnerable (VU)	At high risk of extinction in the wild
Near Threatened (NT)	Likely to become threatened in the near future
Least Concern (LC)	Widespread, abundant, or at low risk
Data Deficient (DD)	Not enough data to make a judgment about the species
Not Evaluated (NE)	Not yet evaluated against the criteria

In the United States, the Endangered Species Act of 1973 was passed to protect species from possible **extinction**. It has its own criteria for classifying species, but they are similar to those of the IUCN. Canada introduced the Species at Risk Act in 2002. More than 530 species are protected under the act. The list of species is compiled by the Committee on the Status of Endangered Wildlife in Canada (COSEWIC).

ALLIGATORS AT RISK

Today, the IUCN Red List classifies the American alligator as Least Concern (LC). The U.S. Endangered Species Act of 1973 named the American alligator as being endangered. After successful conservation efforts, it was removed from the list of endangered and threatened species in 1986.

Joining the Red List

Early European settlers did not like alligators. Farmers worried they would attack valuable livestock, such as cattle. There were no laws to protect animals from hunting, so they killed as many alligators as they wanted. Alligator hunting was especially common in Louisiana and Florida. Hunters killed alligators for meat, and to sell alligator skin for leather. Oil made from alligator fat was also sold and used to **lubricate** machines, such as steam engines. Meanwhile, farmers drained wetlands to grow crops, so the alligators' habitat shrunk. Alligator numbers dropped so rapidly from hunting and habitat loss that eventually they were listed as Endangered.

Alligators suffered as natural wetlands and swamps, such as the Everglades in Florida, were drained. Settlers moving into the region used the wetlands for farming or for building settlements.

In the late 1800s, hunters killed thousands of alligators a month to keep up with the demand for alligator skin.

SKINS IN DEMAND

Alligator skin was commonly used to make boots and saddles. In fact, alligator-skin boots and saddles were used by Confederate soldiers during the American Civil War (1861–1865). Alligator-leather shoes, handbags, belts, and suitcases became fashionable, especially in France. Alligators were also hunted for their meat, which is still eaten today (below right). The invention of the **airboat** in the early 1900s made it even easier to hunt in swamps where alligators lurked. At the same time, people were building homes, farms, and towns on the alligators' habitat. By the mid 1900s, the number of alligators was at its lowest ever. Hunting was made illegal in most states by 1962. Even then, hunting continued, as did **smuggling** and an illegal trade in alligator skins.

An Ecosystem in Danger

The alligator is a **keystone species** that helps keep the wetland ecosystem balanced. The alligators' hunting habits help keep the numbers of other animals under control. Younger alligators hunt insects, fish, and rodents, and adults prey on snakes, mammals, and birds near the water's edge. When the alligator population is low, there are more small animals in the wetlands. They eat birds' eggs, so there are fewer birds in the ecosystem. Alligator homes and movement patterns also benefit other animals. Alligators make water "roads" as they move from place to place. This spreads fresh water across the wetlands for other animals to use. Without the "roads," the areas of fresh water would be smaller.

Large, web-footed rodents called nutria eat many wetland plants. Alligators eat the nutria, which stops too many wetland plants from being eaten. This maintains the balance of the ecosystem.

Many wetland animals depend on "gator holes." These large ponds are an alligator specialty. Using their snouts, claws, and tails, they make large holes that fill with water. During the dry season or during droughts, gator holes provide a home for fish, turtles, birds, and insects. Alligators make these holes deeper and larger every year.

COLLABORATING FOR A CAUSE

In 2000, the U.S. Congress approved the Comprehensive Everglades Restoration Plan (CERP). The project is a partnership of federal and state agencies, including the National Park Service. It aims to regulate human activity to restore the natural ecosystem of South Florida. Over the years, people have **encroached** upon the natural systems of the Everglades. Building canals and draining water reduced the area of wetland, so there is less room for wildlife. As fewer alligators lived in the Everglades (right), the whole ecosystem suffered. When there are plentiful, healthy alligators, scientists working as part of CERP know the Everglades are healthy again.

Getting Involved

When state fish and wildlife agencies realized that the alligator population had declined steeply, they took the first steps to reduce alligator hunting. Alabama passed anti-hunting laws in 1941. Other states, such as Florida, followed in the 1960s. Texas, North Carolina, and South Carolina passed protection laws in 1970. But alligator skins were in high demand, so illegal alligator trading continued.

In the early 1960s, the U.S. government published the Federal Endangered Species list, which included the American alligator. Then, in 1973, President Richard Nixon signed the Endangered Species Act (ESA) into law. The act directed federal bodies such as the National Park Service to figure out ways to help protect the animals listed on the ESA.

Today, alligator hunting is allowed in states such as Louisiana (below). However, it is tightly regulated. Hunters must have a **permit** to be allowed to hunt alligators.

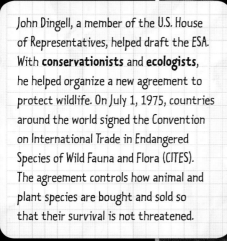

John Dingell, a member of the U.S. House of Representatives, helped draft the ESA. With **conservationists** and **ecologists**, he helped organize a new agreement to protect wildlife. On July 1, 1975, countries around the world signed the Convention on International Trade in Endangered Species of Wild Fauna and Flora (CITES). The agreement controls how animal and plant species are bought and sold so that their survival is not threatened.

COLLABORATING FOR A CAUSE

In 1971, the International Union for Conservation of Nature created a special committee called the Species Survival Commission (IUCN-SSC) Crocodile Specialist Group. It focuses on protecting crocodilians. At the time, all 23 species of crocodilian were endangered or at risk, including the American alligator and the Nile crocodile (below). The commission members were specialists such as biologists, farmers, researchers, and government workers. They came from all over the world to work together to protect the American alligator. Today, the commission has 450 members. The group relies on gifts of money to help its work.

An Action Plan for the Alligator

Putting laws into place to prevent overhunting was the first part of the effort to save the alligator. Some states used laws to ensure that hunters only killed adult alligators, whereas others banned hunting in certain areas and at certain times of the year. However, hunters unhappy with the new laws engaged in **poaching**.

None of the state laws introduced in the 1940s and 1950s helped the alligator population to grow enough. Eventually, officials decided a complete ban on hunting was necessary. In 1962, **commercial** alligator hunting was made illegal everywhere in the United States. Authorities also began to enforce laws that stopped people from buying and selling illegally hunted animals between states.

Scientists at the Rockefeller Wildlife **Refuge** in Louisiana capture young alligators to check their health. They track how many young are being born and the number that grow to adulthood, when they can breed themselves.

COLLABORATING FOR A CAUSE

An important part of the alligator action plan was to understand the creatures better, so that scientists would learn what they needed to survive. The Louisiana Department of Wildlife and Fisheries began an alligator research program in 1959, based at the Rockefeller Wildlife Refuge (below right). The refuge is a large area of coastal marshland that is ideal habitat for alligators. Over many years, the researchers studied wild and captive alligators' behavior, habitat, and diet. One area of research involved capturing and **marking** wild alligators so that the scientists could identify individual animals and track their movements. Another part of the research involved seeing if it was possible for alligators to thrive in captivity on special farms. This might help repopulate them in the wild. Finally, the biologists looked at ways to manage the alligator population in the wild so it did not grow too large.

An alligator's jaws are taped closed while it is studied.

Making the Plan Work

Protecting alligators required the efforts of many different people and organizations. For example, conservationists had to come up with plans to preserve wetland ecosystems. Law enforcement officers had to make sure people followed the new laws. They had to look out for illegal hunting and make arrests. Poachers faced heavy fines and possible jail sentences if they were caught. Today, alligator hunting is allowed again in many places, but laws still control when alligators are hunted and how many alligators are allowed to be killed. Some state laws, for example, make sure that hunting does not threaten alligator eggs, allowing more alligators to survive.

Alligator farms were originally set up to provide skins to make leather. Today, many alligator farms add to their income by allowing tourists to visit.

SAFE REFUGES

As part of the alligator recovery plan, refuges have been set up where the animals can breed and live safely. One of the refuges is Rockefeller Wildlife Refuge in Louisiana. In Florida, alligators live in the Loxahatchee National Wildlife Refuge. They also live in the Alligator River National Wildlife Refuge in North Carolina.

UNEXPECTED SOURCE OF HELP

One unexpected source of help for the recovery of the alligator comes from alligator farms. These farms are businesses that raise alligators to supply alligator meat and skins for the leather **industry**. State departments of wildlife and fisheries work closely with alligator farms to ensure that they help with conservation efforts. Female alligators lay between 35 and 50 eggs, but most do not hatch in the wild. Other animals eat them. Alligator farmers remove eggs from the nests of wild alligators and **incubate** them until they hatch (right). The farmers raise the alligators for two years. At this point, they return about 20 percent of the alligators to the wild. This means that about 20 alligators are released into the wild for every 100 eggs the farmers take.

RAISING AWARENESS

Animal protection groups have supported the protection of the American alligator. Campaigns by organizations such as People for the Ethical Treatment of Animals (PETA) have helped to reduce the demand for fashion products made from alligator skin. PETA campaigns by using advertisements, protests, letters, speeches, and more. In the past, PETA has painted human models as crocodiles and alligators (left) as part of its protests.

Challenges and Solutions

The fight to save the American alligator faced many problems, such as illegal hunting. The government agencies involved knew that to enforce the hunting laws, they had to educate the public about them. They published information and put up signs to inform people about alligator habitats. Even so, people continue to mistreat alligators. To avoid this, states have strict permit laws. It is illegal to own, kill, or capture an alligator without a permit. While other endangered species have been saved by relocating them, this has not been successful for the alligator. It needs to live in wetlands, which exist only in certain areas—and are disappearing. Alligators also have strong "homing" instincts, which means they naturally find their way back home even from far away.

Alligator wrestling is a popular sport in some regions. It is one of the traditions of the Seminole people in Florida. However, groups such as the Animal Rights Foundation of Florida argue that the sport is cruel and harms the alligator.

ALLIGATORS IN THE BACKYARD

Many alligators live in wildlife refuges or parks, where hunting is easily controlled. However, as homes and cities are built on or near wetland habitats, some alligators live on land owned by regular people. It is difficult to prevent them from hunting alligators on their own land. In Florida, however, the Fish and Wildlife Conservation Commission came up with a plan. Before alligators are allowed to be removed from private properties, biologists look at the number of alligators and how healthy they are. The biologists write a report and determine the number of animals or eggs that can safely be removed (right).

People have built canals through the Everglades and other swamps. The canals take much of the water from the surrounding land, which dries out. This leaves less wetland habitat for the alligators and other wildlife.

Return of the Alligator

The efforts to bring the American alligator back from the brink have succeeded. Hunting has been controlled. Alligator farming has also helped increase the population by releasing young alligators into the wild. In Louisiana, there were fewer than 200,000 alligators in 1970. By 1993, there were almost one million. Today, there are about two million. As the number of alligators grew, the Fish and Wildlife Service began to remove them from the list of endangered species. In 1987, the American alligator was fully **delisted**. Today, there are about five million alligators in the southeastern United States. The recovery of the alligators has helped wetland ecosystems. Alligators eat many nutria, so more water plants grow and provide food for other species. In addition, alligator nests are reused by animals such as turtles. Gator holes hold water for other animals even through long dry periods.

A dead alligator is pulled onboard a boat during an alligator hunt in the Atchafalaya Basin in Louisiana.

MONITORING ALLIGATORS

Experts monitor the American alligator population and give advice to the U.S. Fish and Wildlife Service and state governments. The Croc Docs are a team of biologists from the University of Florida who work in the South and in the Caribbean. Their projects include monitoring alligators in the Florida Everglades in order to check that the ecosystem is healthy. They also remove dangerous alligators. One of their priorities is educating people about ways in which they can live safely alongside alligators.

ALLIGATOR RANGE, 2018

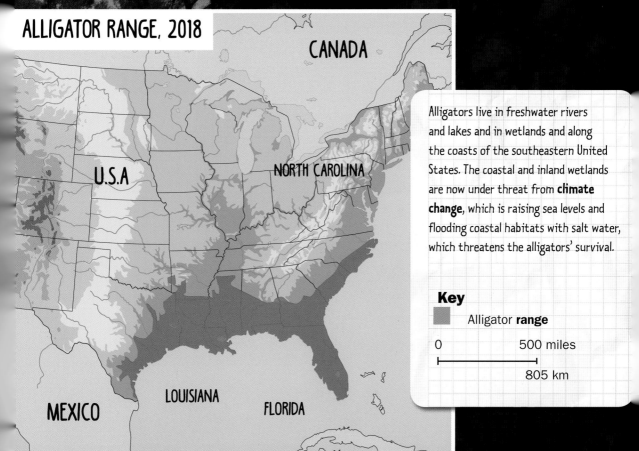

CANADA

NORTH CAROLINA

U.S.A

MEXICO

LOUISIANA

FLORIDA

Alligators live in freshwater rivers and lakes and in wetlands and along the coasts of the southeastern United States. The coastal and inland wetlands are now under threat from **climate change**, which is raising sea levels and flooding coastal habitats with salt water, which threatens the alligators' survival.

Key

Alligator **range**

0   500 miles

805 km

Healing the Ecosystem

Alligators are now widespread across the southeastern United States. However, it will take a long time for places such as the Everglades to fully recover. Alligators are doing their part. Their gator holes and hunting habits are slowly helping to restore ecosystems. More alligators also mean more nests. Alligators make their large nests from plants and mud. Over time, the plants break down, and these nests become peat. Peatlands are very important, because they provide healthy habitats for many plants and animals. Peat also takes in harmful carbon dioxide from the air and stores the carbon underground. This helps to protect the environment from climate change.

Birds and alligators may be natural enemies, but they help each other. Alligators lurk under birds' nests, keeping away other predators, such as raccoons. Alligators feed on weak chicks and eggs that fall from nests.

COLLABORATING FOR A CAUSE

State agencies, conservationists, and environmental groups all work together to protect the alligator and its habitat, and to manage the trade in alligator skins and meat. They manage the alligator population in the wild. Alligators are an **indicator species**. This means scientists can understand an environment by studying the alligators that live there. For example, biologists study the health of Everglades alligators. Unhealthy alligators might show that the environment is unhealthy. In this case, experts try to figure what the problem is and how to improve it. Meanwhile, both CITES and the ESA have laws to make sure that American alligators, or their skins or meat, are not traded illegally. Every alligator that is killed has a plastic CITES tag punched into its tail. This allows every animal to be tracked and counted, so that they are not overhunted.

Biologists study a tranquilized American alligator in the Everglades. If an animal is sick, it might indicate that the fresh water of the swamp is mixed with salt water or that there is a shortage of food. Wildlife management teams try to solve such problems.

What Does the Future Hold?

The American alligator population is high again in the wild, but alligators remain at risk from people. They are still hunted illegally or killed by accident. Many cities are built on or near alligator habitats, which causes alligators to have higher encounters with humans. Many alligators that encounter humans are killed. Alligators do not attack people very often, because they have a natural fear of people. However, attacks do happen. Female alligators fiercely guard their nests. If people get too close, these mothers may attack to protect their young. Other alligators have lost their fear of people and associate them with food. At other times, people tease an alligator by throwing things at it. Alligators may attack if they are provoked in this way.

As more cities are built on or near wetlands, more people encroach on alligator habitats. This cyclist takes a photograph as an alligator crosses a bicycle trail in Florida.

HABITATS UNDER THREAT

The alligators' wetland habitat is at risk from people and climate change. People have destroyed the alligators' natural habitat by clearing trees and plants or draining water routes. People also release **toxins** into the water. Farms near wetlands often use **pesticides** in their fields, which run off into wetlands. The chemicals make the alligators sick or unable to grow properly. If farmers use more natural methods to treat their crops, alligators will be healthier. Climate change also threatens wetlands, which are vulnerable to hurricanes and rising water levels. In low-lying coastal wetlands, such as Florida, salt water enters the waterways, making it difficult for alligators to live there. Experts restoring the wetlands try to increase the flow of fresh water there.

Global warming has led to higher temperatures around the world. These changes affect the alligator population in the southeastern United States. The temperature around an alligator egg determines if the young alligator will be male or female. Higher temperatures breed more male alligators. Fewer female alligators means that fewer eggs are laid in the years to come, lowering the alligator population.

Saving Other Species

Many crocodilians are still endangered around the world. The IUCN lists seven crocodilians as critically endangered. One of the most endangered is the Chinese alligator. In 2002, China developed an action plan to save the alligator. As in the United States, the Chinese plan focused on research, education, and habitat. Even so, the Chinese alligator remains critically endangered. It has lost much of its habitat, and there are very few in the wild. Many Chinese alligators were also killed when they encountered humans. China is working to restore the habitat. The National Chinese Alligator Natural Reserve breeds and protects the alligator.

The Chinese alligator's wetland habitat was used by humans for growing rice. Today, there are only about 150 individuals in the wild and another 100 in captivity.

THE GHARIAL

Before the mid-1900s, thousands of crocodilian gharials (below right) lived in rivers in South Asia, but their numbers fell dramatically due to overhunting. In the early 1970s, conservation efforts began in **sanctuaries** and breeding centers. Even so, the number of wild gharials fell to fewer than 200 by 2006.

The Gharial Conservation Alliance (GCA) is based in India. It works to protect the gharial's habitat. The loss of habitat remains a problem for crocodilians around the world. Today, the IUCN lists the gharial as Critically Endangered.

The American crocodile is threatened, due to hunting and habitat loss. Only about 1,000 wild crocodiles remain in the United States. Luckily, efforts to protect the American alligator, such as hunting laws, also extend to protect the American crocodile. The IUCN listed the crocodile as Endangered, but in 1994, it raised its status to Vulnerable, thanks to successful conservation plans.

What Can You Do to Help?

You can help protect the American alligator, even if where you live is not home to alligators. You can participate in and teach others about environmentally friendly practices, such as reducing waste, that help protect ecosystems. Learn as much as you can about alligators and crocodiles, and speak out about the problems they face. If you can, visit an alligator refuge to see the animals up close. Use websites from organizations such as the IUCN to find out about current conservation programs.

Protecting wetlands is one of the most effective ways to help the American alligator. Wetlands are shrinking as humans change the landscape. The Everglades wetlands have shrunk by more than half of their original size over the last 100 years.

Respect the Alligator

If you live in or visit a southern state, you might get to see real alligators in the wild. Never approach them or try to touch them. If possible, visit alligators in a safe environment, such as a wildlife park. Wherever you see an alligator, do not try to feed it. Feeding alligators is illegal. If alligators get used to being fed, they may begin to approach people for food. This will bring alligators into more contact with humans, which can be dangerous for people and often results in the alligator being captured and killed.

Alligators are cold-blooded. This means they rely on sunlight or water to make their bodies warmer or cooler. They often lie out in the sunlight to get warm. Their mouths might be open to release some heat if they are too warm.

KEEP HABITATS HEALTHY

The wetlands where the American alligator lives are just one of North America's endangered habitats. Pollution and spreading towns and cities threaten the wilderness. Help to protect wildlife and nature by following the steps below:

- Never litter, and always recycle when you can.

- Do not waste water, and always be careful what you put into sinks and drains. Chemicals or tiny pieces of plastic can get into rivers and lakes, and eventually cause harm to wetland plants and animals such as the American alligator.

- Volunteer to help to plant trees. Trees help to keep the air and water clean. This helps to keep the wetland habitats healthy.

Learning More

Books

Feigenbaum, Aaron. *American Alligators: Freshwater Survivors.* Bearport Publishing Company, 2008.

Hirsch, Rebecca E. *American Alligators: Armored Roaring Reptiles. Comparing Animal Traits.* Lerner Publications, 2016.

Mooney, Carla. *American Alligator. Back from Near Extinction*. Minneapolis: Core Library, 2017.

Nagle, Jeanne. *Saving the Endangered American Alligator*. Britannica Educational Publishing, 2016.

On the Web

www.biokids.umich.edu/critters/ Alligator_mississippiensis
Learn detailed information about alligators, such as their communication habits, how they grow, and what they eat.

www.iucncsg.org/pages/Major-Conservation-Initiatives.html
Browse the IUCN Crocodile Specialist Group page on the latest conservation efforts to protect crocodilian species.

myfwc.com/media/310155/ alligator-aaa-booklet.pdf
Check out this downloadable activity book with information about and drawings of American alligators, from the Florida Fish and Wildlife Commission.

crocdoc.ifas.ufl.edu
This University of Florida site is about wildlife researchers known as the "Croc Docs," who specialize in alligator and crocodile research and management. Read about their current and past projects, and check out the fact sheets and brochures.

CRABTREE Plus

For videos, activities, and more, enter the access code at the Crabtree Plus website below.

www.crabtreeplus.com/animals-back-brink

Access code: abb37

Glossary

airboat A boat with an aircraft engine, used in swamps

apex predator An animal that has no natural predators

captivity Being kept in a place and not being allowed to leave

carnivores Animals that eat mainly meat

climate change A change in normal global weather patterns thought to be caused in part by human activity

commercial Carried out as a business to make money

conservation The preserving and protecting of plants, animals, and natural resources

conservationist An expert in conservation

cultivation The deliberate breeding and growing of plants, such as crops

decline Fall in number

delist To remove a species from the Endangered Species List

ecologists Scientists who study the relationships between living things and their environment

ecosystem Everything that exists in a particular environment, including animals and plants and nonliving things, such as soil and sunlight

encroached Moved into territory already used by someone or something

endangered In danger of becoming extinct

habitats The natural surroundings in which animals live

incubate To keep eggs warm so they will hatch

indicator species A species that reflects the health of an ecosystem

industry The processing of raw materials or the manufacturing of goods

keystone species An animal on which other animals and plants in a particular ecosystem depend

lubricate To use oil to make parts of a machine run smoothly

marking Attaching a tag or other form of identification to an animal

natural resources Useful materials that occur in nature

permit A licence to do something

pesticides Chemicals used to kill bugs and weeds

poaching Hunting, catching, or killing animals illegally

range The geographical area in which an animal usually lives

refuge Protected area or place for animals to live

reptiles Animals with scaly skin that lay their eggs on land

sanctuaries Places where wildlife is protected

settlers A person who arrives in a new place, often from another country, to live there and use the land

smuggling Transporting and selling goods illegally

species A group of similar animals or plants that can breed with one another

toxins Poisonous substances

wetlands A damp ecosystem consisting of swamps and marshes

Index and About the Author

ABOUT THE AUTHOR

Cynthia O'Brien has written many nonfiction books for children and young readers. She first became fascinated by alligators after a visit to the Florida Everglades.